Captures from Cathy's Camera

CATHY JEAN PALMER

Captures from Cathy's Camera

ABOUT THE AUTHOR

Cathy Jean Palmer has been living in Panama City Beach, Florida, since 2010, enjoying every minute as her children and grandchildren live here too. Her hobbies besides photography are walking on the beach, collecting seashells, riding her bike to St Andrews State Park and blogging. When you have a few, check out her I DIG THE BEACH blog at idigthebeach.blogspot.com. Contact Cathy via email at cathyjpalmer@yahoo.com